First Facts®

Spotlight on the Continents

SPOTLIGHT ON
EUROPE

by Karen Bush Gibson

CAPSTONE PRESS
a capstone imprint

First Facts is published by Capstone Press,
151 Good Counsel Drive, P.O. Box 669, Mankato, Minnesota 56002.
www.capstonepub.com

Books published by Capstone Press are manufactured with paper
containing at least 10 percent post-consumer waste.

Library of Congress Cataloging-in-Publication Data
Gibson, Karen Bush.
  Spotlight on Europe / by Karen Bush Gibson.
    p. cm.—(First facts. Spotlight on the continents)
  Summary: "An introduction to Europe including climate, landforms, plants, animals,
and people"—Provided by publisher.
  Includes bibliographical references and index.
  ISBN 978-1-4296-6625-1 (library binding)
  1. Europe—Juvenile literature. I. Title.
  D1051.G57 2011
  940—dc22   2010037111

Editorial Credits
Lori Shores, editor; Gene Bentdahl, designer; Laura Manthe, production specialist

Photo Credits
Corel, cover, 1
image100, 14 (bottom)
Shutterstock/Elena Elisseeva, 13; Mark Dyer, 14 (top); Norbert Derec, 9; Rob Wilson, 20;
    Stanislav Sokolov, 12; Tupungato, 16, 19

Artistic Effects
Shutterstock/seed

Essential content terms are **bold** and are defined at the bottom of the page
where they first appear.

Printed in the United States of America in Melrose Park, Illinois.
092010   005935LKS11

TABLE OF CONTENTS

CONTINENTS OF THE WORLD

EUROPE

Europe is the second smallest **continent** in the world. It only covers about 4 million square miles (10.4 million square kilometers). But Europe has helped shape many countries. European history, art, and buildings interest people all over the world.

continent—one of Earth's seven large landmasses

FAST FACTS ABOUT
EUROPE

🌐 **Population:** About 707 million

🌐 **Number of countries:** 49

🌐 **Largest cities:** Moscow, Russia; London, United Kingdom; Paris, France

🌐 **Highest point:** Mount Elbrus, 18,510 feet (5,642 meters) above sea level

🌐 **Lowest point:** shore of the Caspian Sea, 92 feet (28 meters) below sea level

🌐 **Longest river:** Volga River, 2,194 miles (3,531 kilometers) long

COUNTRIES OF EUROPE

CLIMATE

Warm ocean winds keep most of Europe's **climate** from getting too cold. Dry southern countries rarely get below freezing. But Europe does have cold spots. Snow and ice cover parts of Iceland and northern Europe all year.

climate—the usual weather that occurs in a place

LANDFORMS OF EUROPE

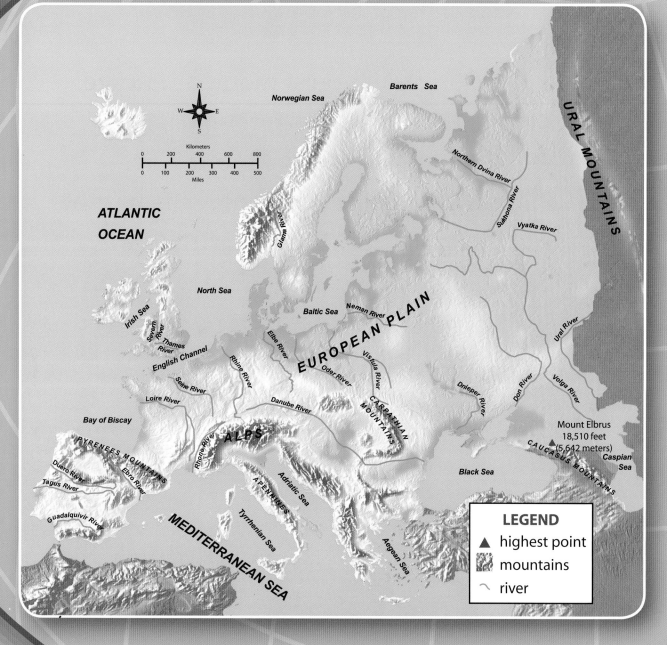

ATLANTIC OCEAN

Norwegian Sea

Barents Sea

URAL MOUNTAINS

Northern Dvina River

Sukhona River

Vyatka River

Glama River

North Sea

Baltic Sea

Neman River

EUROPEAN PLAIN

Ural River

Irish Sea

Severn River

Thames River

English Channel

Elbe River

Oder River

Vistula River

Rhine River

Seine River

Loire River

Danube River

CARPATHIAN MOUNTAINS

Dnieper River

Don River

Volga River

Bay of Biscay

PYRENEES MOUNTAINS

Rhone River

ALPS

Mount Elbrus
18,510 feet
(5,642 meters)

CAUCASUS MOUNTAINS

Caspian Sea

Duero River

Ebro River

Tagus River

APENNINES

Adriatic Sea

Black Sea

Guadalquivir River

Tyrrhenian Sea

MEDITERRANEAN SEA

Aegean Sea

Kilometers
0   200   400   600   800
0   100 200 300 400 500
Miles

LEGEND
▲ highest point
mountains
⌒ river

10

LANDFORMS

Europe's largest mountain **range**, the Alps, stretches through seven southern countries. Mount Elbrus, Europe's highest mountain, is part of the Caucasus Mountains in Russia.

Crops grow on the flat European Plain. Farmers use Europe's longest river, the Volga, to water crops.

range—a chain or large group of mountains
crop—a plant grown in large amounts that is often used for food

PLANTS

Europe's mixed climate is perfect for growing many crops. Farmers grow grains and potatoes in Western Europe's warm climate.

Olives and grapes grow in hot, dry areas. Evergreen trees fill large forests in cool areas. Few plants grow in the cold mountains.

ANIMALS

Europe's forests, mountains, and waters are home to many animals. Reindeer and other large animals live in open areas. Small animals, such as squirrels, rabbits, and foxes, are common all over Europe. Swans and ducks nest near lakes and ponds. Playful apes climb rocks in Spain.

POPULATION DENSITY OF EUROPE

People per
square mile

People per
square kilometer

Less than 2	Less than 1
2 to 25	1 to 10
25 to 125	10 to 50
125 to 250	50 to 100
More than 250	More than 100

• major cities/urban centers
More than 7.5 million people

N W E S

•MOSCOW

LONDON•

ATLANTIC OCEAN

•PARIS

EUROPE

•ISTANBUL

ASIA

AFRICA

PEOPLE

Most people speak more than one language in Europe. Across Europe, more than 50 languages are spoken. English, French, and German are the most common.

Christianity has been the main religion in Europe for hundreds of years. Other religions practiced in Europe include Judaism and Islam.

LIVING IN EUROPE

Most people in Europe live in houses or apartments. In many countries, more than half of the people live in cities. Fewer people live on farms and in cold northern areas.

People enjoy a variety of foods in Europe. Switzerland is known for its cheese and chocolate. People eat sausages with sauerkraut in Germany. Italy is known for its pizza and pasta.

EUROPE AND THE WORLD

Europe has given much to the world. **Democracy** and legal systems are based on European ideas. Many countries around the world have based their education systems and art styles on ideas from this continent.

democracy—a government in which people choose their leaders by voting

GLOSSARY

climate (KLY-muht)—the usual weather that occurs in a place

continent (KAHN-tuh-nuhnt)—one of Earth's seven large landmasses

crop (KROP)—a plant grown in large amounts that is often used for food

democracy (di-MAH-kruh-see)—a government in which people choose their leaders by voting

range (RAYNJ)—a chain or large group of mountains

READ MORE

Aloian, Molly, and Bobbie Kalman. *Explore Europe.* Explore the Continents. New York: Crabtree Pub. Co., 2007.

Bingham, Jane. *Europe.* Exploring Continents. Chicago: Heinemann Library, 2007.

Foster, Karen. *Atlas of Europe.* World Atlases. Minneapolis: Picture Window Books, 2008.

INTERNET SITES

FactHound offers a safe, fun way to find Internet sites related to this book. All of the sites on FactHound have been researched by our staff.

Here's all you do:

Visit *www.facthound.com*

Type in this code: 9781429666251

Check out projects, games and lots more at
www.capstonekids.com

INDEX